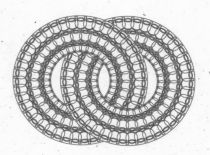

Set in Stone

Set in Stone

Kevin Carey

CAVANKERRY PRESS

CavanKerry Press Ltd.
Fort Lee, New Jersey
www.cavankerrypress.org

Publisher's Cataloging-In-Publication Data
(Prepared by The Donohue Group, Inc.)
Names: Carey, Kevin, 1957- author.
Title: Set in stone / Kevin Carey.
Other Titles: Emerging voices series.
Description: First edition. | Fort Lee, New Jersey : CavanKerry Press Ltd., 2020.
Identifiers: ISBN 9781933880792
Subjects: LCSH: Memory—Poetry. | Nostalgia—Poetry. | Loss (Psychology)—Poetry. | Aging—Psychological aspects—Poetry. | LCGFT: Poetry.
Classification: LCC PS3603.A7416 S48 2020 | DDC 811/.6—dc23

Cover and interior text design by Mayfly Design
First Edition 2020, Printed in the United States of America

CavanKerry Press is grateful for the support it receives from the New Jersey State Council on the Arts.

Also by Kevin Carey

The One Fifteen to Penn Station (2012)
The Beach People (2014)
Jesus Was a Homeboy (2016)

for my dad

Contents

III

Set in Stone

Story

I forfeit false promises
I wishfully imagine
I am desperate
I am insufferable rebellious
I am a red ant
I am layers of ice
I am birds I am fish I am a water bug
I am blind
I am opulent (always in flux)
I am obsolete
fantastic dizzy
I am no simple answer

Memory

It's like being locked out of the theater
when your favorite movie is playing:
You know the film
you know it's on the big screen in there
you know the scenes
some of the lines by heart
but you can't hear the projector purring
you can't feel the strangers around you
munching popcorn
so you stare into the lobby
past the girl with the glasses in the ticket window
past the Sold Out sign
past the old man sweeping the floor
and you think *I know that guy*
and the marquee over your head goes dark
and a slight rain makes you shiver
and you shuffle your feet on the damp sidewalk
and you hope you see someone leaving
after the show so you can ask *was it good?*

Picking Up the Trail

It wasn't that long ago when I'd stop at the stairs
and catch my kids jumping to the floor.
Now I drop them at airports and bus stations,
or watch them drive their cars away
packed with blankets and suitcases.

When they are gone, I think of them sitting
in some coffee shop laughing with their friends
or standing in a crowded barroom at night
telling funny stories from back home:
my dad says, come on! *when he gets mad.*

I picture them walking through their own
neighborhoods turning back and looking
as if I'm following them on horseback
across an empty open desert,
a tired Pinkerton man on the trail of yesterday.

The Tobin Bridge

For Pam

I have friends who are afraid
of crossing bridges.
It panics them to drive
with the world spreading out
on either side of them.

I know this fear—like so many
of my own, it is linked
to the worst of our imagination.

I have a recurring dream
about driving on a suspended
bridge, arched with a deck
over the ocean—

the more I drive in the dream,
the steeper it gets, until my car
is almost upside down, and
always, just before it flips, I wake.

I am reminded of that dream today
crossing the Sagamore to Cape Cod,
still numb from the image back home,
our friend Pam standing against the dark
and stepping into nothingness.

After we heard, we lay in bed remembering
as if she'd been gone for years—
the trip we took to Ireland, her loaded
down with shopping bags in Glengarriff,
the kind way she had with our kids,
her love affair with the Red Sox.

My wife helped her so often over
the years and I remember getting
exasperated once when I was
told of another episode,
not because I wasn't sympathetic,
but because I was frightened.

I remember thinking *that could be me.*

We're all so close to it, aren't we,
clinging to that tenuous support,
that bridge to sanity that keeps
us suspended over what could be?

This is how I see it:
she is flying, not falling,
the lights of downtown Boston
are reflecting in the soft snowfall,
her eyes are closed, the hum of the traffic
has faded, her arms, like wings, lift her
over the harbor, and in that moment,
she knows much more than we know.

Concord

I stop in Concord Center
on my way to read at a federal prison.
My grandmother's cottage on nearby
White Pond was sold years ago.
We used to pack up the car and drive
from Revere along Route 16
past the two-families in Medford
until we crossed the cow pastures
and the Concord River.
In those days I'd swim
from one side of the pond to the other
chasing frogs from the wet brush
and watching the moths at night
circling the lamplight like men
I'd seen around a barrel of burning trash.
Today I walk the same sidewalks where my father
took me to breakfast, where I bought
Tiny Buttons (cherry and lime) at the five and ten.
I think of being twelve years old and cutting
into a pancake and talking with him
about Bill Russell or some other Celtic
or a movie we watched, a western
maybe or a monster flick with Boris Karloff.

I stop in a local bookstore and buy a book of poems
by Gerald Stern and spend an hour reading
and remembering like he does, old cars and old faces.
The poems make me think of high school,
the time I drove here in my brother-in-law's
green Torino with my friend Ed
to drink beer all day and steal baloney
from the local supermarket,

and that one August afternoon
when I went swimming with Judee Rainville
and we fell asleep on the raft in the late day sun.

By the time I leave for the prison up Route 2,
the nostalgia has become the natural ghost
and I'm reminded of the dream about being molested,
here in the woods by the family cottage,
by a man I couldn't recognize, only the long
arms of a red checkered shirt wrapped around me.

I asked my family about it—my brother, my mother
before she couldn't remember anything.
Now there's no one to ask anymore.

I'm near the prison after going the wrong way
and having to double back and the closer I get
the more the pretty visions of my childhood
seem to slip through my fingers like the slimy
green frogs of summer and I'm left with
my own haunted fears, real or imagined,
and I'm kicking and crawling through the warm
pond water, my arms outstretched,
reaching toward the other side.

Thirteen Ways of Looking at a Blackboard

I

Hold my lines and my circles,
smooth and black and everything.

II

Fingerprints, shades of old writing.
Things disappearing.

III

My fingernails tapping then
screeching from top to bottom.

IV

Answer the problem on the board, she demands.
I didn't do the homework.
Death row steps.

V

Every image a silent movie.

VI

Michael Ferragamo, who stayed back
three times, dents the cool slate
behind me with a desk meant for my head.

VII

A warm September day: open windows, hot air,
and chalk dust floating. I hear kickball on the
playground writing one hundred times.

VIII

I will not blow spitballs at Michael
I will not blow spitballs at Michael
I will not blow spitballs at Michael

IX

Miss Collintino called me stupid. The chalk broke in my hand.

X

When she writes in chalk, I watch her hair bounce.
The way she reaches on her tiptoes, every scrolled word an invitation.

XI

Years later I stand with my back to you
students trying to read my writing,
I'll explain, I say. *Don't worry.*

XII

The American Revolution, fractions, Penmanship.
Is there anything you can't do?

XIII

Mr. Pulo rolls up the map of the Soviet Union to discover a chalk drawing
of a penis.

West Palm

The blue bar door open
quarts of beer on the pool table
sirens up and down West Dixie
sweat-soaked walls
cockroaches
a gunshot across the hall
more orange tickets
on the windshield of a car
an open empty trunk
everything gone
and a mile away
the Kennedys throw a bash
and the ocean washes up
on a stone patio
gin fizzes and fashion shows
palm trees
a golf course
a movie star
and a young man
gray shirt and pants
rolling a ten-foot table
down an empty hallway
on the midnight shift.

Reunion

I see her with a group of students
coming into the room—
an adult in a day class.
(They always stick out.)
She recognizes me.
I knew her in high school.
Her hair is dyed blonde now.
She's too thin.
Her father was my basketball coach.
I flashback to the undefeated run,
the after parties.
She waves me into the hall
and starts talking
but it's hard to understand her.
She points to her throat—
ALS, she says, *my tongue doesn't work.*
She tells me they gave her two to five years.
She's in year two.
She wants to finish her degree.
She tells me she needs a feeding tube,
she can't swallow.
She spits into a coffee cup.
I remember my buddy from Brooklyn
who dated her, and her curly-haired friend
from the Willows, my prom date,
the time the four of us wandered
into Fantasy Island stoned
and ran out when we saw her father.
She tells me she just went to a 40th
reunion. I can picture it,
her classmates straining to listen,
whispering later with drinks

and cocktail napkins in their hands,
secretly feeling lucky they're not her.
Before she goes back to her class,
she says, *I always talked so much*
maybe someone wanted me to finally
shut the fuck up.
We both laugh at that.

Night Swimming, Assumption College—1979

They call it *the duck pond,*
lily pads, wild grass, and sprigs
of daisies around the edge.
The breeze makes circles
of the dark water,
skeeters skimming across
on paper legs and a gang
of boys in their underwear
jumping in together,
resurfacing with a breast stroke,
or a crawl, a collective scream,
their beer cans floating to the surface.
They pile out laughing,
running up the grassy hill,
all but one,
a redhead, still and silent,
everything gone numb.
He thinks *don't leave me*
as the raucous voices fade
across campus.

But they do.

The Charlestown Boys Club Tournament—1970

We lose in the semifinals
to a team from Swampscott.
I cry in the locker room—
still young enough to hate
the idea of losing.

After, we drive over the bridge
in my father's Buick Skylark
the smoke across the green iron grate
past the brick three-families
the rooftops strung with clothes
like the masts of pirate ships.

I hum the tune "Homeward Bound"
and remember the gray cap
I bought to look like Paul Simon
on the seat beside me.

The Swampscott team was much better:
they passed the ball, trapped on defense,
got easy shots. We struggled to
score, but a few times I crossed over
to the hoop for a basket,
made a couple of jumpers.

I smile thinking—
as my father drives
along the beach, past the stands
boarded up for the winter—
how much I love basketball,
playing in dark little gyms

that smell like dust and chlorine,
flying ahead of the pack for a breakaway,
watching a long-range jump shot
hang in the air for hours.

The Curse

Okay here's the thing:
I've got a list of regrets
dating back a thousand years—
the should-have could-have
haunts that cloud my thinking
when I'm driving home alone
from school or crossing
the Tappan Zee on my way north,
that thing I said, the wrong time
to have the last drink, the time
in junior high at the bowling alley
or that day at Sabbaday Falls
(25 feet onto a rock)—

the few too many nights
I would gladly trade in for time served.

It all comes down to this:
I was raised Irish Catholic
which means I'm a guilty fucker,
so I regret everything I've done or
everything my ancestors have done.

It's what I need to do daily:
embrace a moment or two of necessary
pain, suffer just a little more than yesterday
so I can eventually be absolved,
walk through purgatory to the pearly
gates, the guilt slipping off my shoulders
like an old cotton shawl.

Super Blue Boy

It's been a long time since I've worn the blue,
the fresh linen flapping,
and those rubber-soled boots.
I jumped mountains for *Christsakes,*
ran with trains just for fun,
swooped onto thirteenth-floor landings
just to say hi. But that girl,
she couldn't take the truth,
too smart for her own good,
not after a freak.
She wanted normal, more than muscles
and shoulders, more than
aerial taxi rides around the city.
So much for superpowers, I guess.

It's been a long time
since this boy in blue flew
like a bullet, like a plane.
You get to be my age
and nothing matters but the girl.

Not Tonight

I'm sitting under a picture of Jesus,
you know the one, the pose where
he's looking down as if he's spotted
something on his sandal. It's Saturday
night at the convent retreat and I am
scribbling another poem, trying to stay
neat with the lines, like a newly readied
Jenga pile. I've moved to a quiet room,
the heat now at sauna level unlike
earlier when I told Maria *it was colder*
than a well digger's ass and I'm feeling
good, really good about being here again,
laughing with old friends, writing poems,
thinking about what Jesus is looking at
on the ground and I realize that for a few
nights they can't get me—the news, the
school, the bill collectors, the projects
back home still undone and nagging me,
the world and all its hate, all its injustice,
all the misogynistic, homophobic, racist
rants. They will all have to wait until
tomorrow afternoon when I pass the old
nun graveyard and the cell phone tower
that looks like a birdhouse. They will know
where to find me when I crawl through
Mendham by the Black Horse Tavern,
or when I'm driving over the new Tappan
Zee Bridge or later on Commonwealth
Ave in Boston. But not tonight. Tonight my
stomach is full, I'm with friends, and I'm
writing poems.

Anna Maria Island

Once the fog clears
I'm left with the harping
of laughing gulls
and pelicans diving
like missiles in the blue-
green ocean.
A boat slows at
the backwater channel,
the Tampa Bay Bridge
a ghost in the distance.
There's a hush here today
in the rippled tide.
I hook my last frozen shrimp
and let it drop beneath the surface
to where the water turns dark,
and I wait,
maybe for a monkfish hiding
in the shadows.
My mom and dad loved
this place—the symphony
of squawking gulls, the grace
of egrets, the wise-eyed pelicans.
They are both gone now
and I'm visiting for the last time
after coming for 30 years.
I hear the clipped leaves
of two palm trees
in the island breeze,
guardians of the slow and easy.
I've come to know
this island life,
everything taking its time,

the sun, the humidity
bringing all of us to a crawl.

I'm thinking of a promise
or the idea of endless beach days
when there's a tug on my line,
my last bit of bait,
all of the memories stolen
in one last frozen moment.

A Dream in Newark

For Bel

We have just stepped off an elevator
I know, always an elevator right
and I am standing frightened
with my hands pressed against
the stone wall of a towering cathedral
and I'm looking out at a quartered
courtyard, lush and flowering,
and I see to my left, my infant son,
diaper and all, moving along the ledge.
I'm reaching for him as I struggle
to hold on, and just when I feel like
I can't balance anymore
we are riding the elevator down,
him safely cooing in my arms.
I have the dream so often
I get comfortable with it
like knowing the ending to
a horror movie—*don't worry: he lives.*
But it's not this dream or the one
about my dead mother singing
at the kitchen sink that haunts me,
it's the other recurring dream,
the one my father had after World War II—
a home, a job, a family—
the one the shuttle driver in Newark
at the Dodge Poetry Festival
talks about. He tells me
now that he's home from Iraq
he doesn't trust the military anymore,
the road to the dream, I think.
He agrees with me about the

illusion of truth no matter which
party is handing it out.
He's happy not to be carrying
a rifle in the desert,
happy to be home with his kid,
but I can tell the dream that haunts him
is the same one a lot of returning vets have,
the one he can't grab no matter
how often he reaches for it.
My father was lucky: he got his,
bartended his way to owning
a piece of a restaurant,
had a state job, helped me
get a piece of mine.
I look out the shuttle window,
police on every corner,
beefed-up patrols for the poetry festival.
I know that Newark,
once a center for tanning and dye work,
has a hard-luck reputation.
I've heard that Down Neck
(on the bend of the Passaic River)
is a safe place for dreams,
but maybe not Lower Roseville
or South Broad Street after dark.
I want to tell the driver to hang
in there, no matter where he lives,
that dreams come true in Newark, too
but I don't—dreaming is easy—
it's waking up that's hard.

Set in Stone

A rosary that was my mother's
tucked in the glove compartment of his car
and a copy of *Exile on Main St.*
with instructions to play track 6
when he hit some lonesome desert highway.
I love him so much my chest hurts,
thinking of him riding off into his own life,
me the weeping shadow left behind (for now).
I know I'll see him again but it's ceremony
we're talking about after all—
one growing up and one growing older
both wild curses.
A train blows its horn,
the light rising beyond the harbor,
a dog barks from a car window,
and the nostalgia (always dangerous)
hits me like a left hook.
I'm trapped between the memory
and the moment,
the deal we make
if we make it this long,
the markers of a life,
the small worthwhile pieces
that rattle around in my pockets,
waiting to be set somewhere in stone.

II

Go West

All *that we see or seem is but a dream within a dream.*
    —Edgar Allan Poe

It's a home movie I haven't shot yet. Someone else shooting me, my twenty-five-year-old son driving us past Haight-Ashbury, along Divisadero Street, a Leonard Cohen song playing,

When Jesus was the honeymoon
and Cain was just the man . . .
the wilderness is gathering
all its children back again.

The windows are open, the sun is setting, there's an autumn cool to this San Francisco late afternoon. My son lives on the other side. The East Bay. We've been visiting for two days. He's been our driver for the weekend. A big step for me, taking the passenger seat. Maybe I'm finally growing up. I'm happy to see him living his life as a young man. I think of Lucinda Williams like I always do in these pensive existential moods. *Come out west and see. . . . / I know you won't stay permanently / but come out west and see.*

He's a West Coast kid (for now anyway). Maybe I'm dreaming of shedding my own East Coast life for the warmer, even more liberal pastures of the Bay Area. I'm taken with the scene out here, the California air, the Pacific, the bay in Oakland, the true hippies.

We listened earlier to a podcast of *Ear Hustle: True Stories from Inside San Quentin Prison,* driving through the marshes of Point Reyes, and picking up I-80. We talked about his volunteering there, working with the forgotten population.

That morning in a bookstore in Emeryville, I picked up a copy of *The New Jim Crow* by Michelle Alexander, and I thought how easy it is to get caught in a corrupt system and how a few bad choices can unjustly affect your whole life. I consider the mistakes I've made, the stupid kid I once was and what didn't matter to me then, and the possible psychic change that comes after figuring a few things out. The idea that you start out in the world one way and end up another is both promising and frightening.

I want what my son wants, some true answers and a purpose.

We spent yesterday driving down the mountains of Stinson Beach, walking the black sand shore, back and forth, no one in a hurry, drinking tea by a park with a big peace sign and a welcome gate made of wood, like the entrance to a temple. These little black birds flitted around our table, and we fed them cookie scraps.

The other night we ate in a restaurant in Berkeley, played a game of hopscotch on the sidewalk utility covers out front. Really, I played it and got my wife to take a turn. A woman walking by stopped and laughed, watched me try it again. I was wearing a Boston Celtics hat but she didn't seem to mind, even though they beat the Warriors a night ago.

The restaurant was all brick, and I ate crab and squid and an apple tart I could have eaten a wagon full of. My son talked about the *inside game*, the money-fueled reality of it. *That's the way they want it,* I said, *a nation divided by race, or region, or religion, so the people won't realize just how powerful they can be.*

It reminded me of something I heard once: if all the spiders in the world realized how many of them there were, they could eat all of us.

But, I said, *you still need to find the joy, so it doesn't crush you.*

We ended up at the movies. A cute story of a girl leaving home for college, out of touch with her parents. It almost made me cry, just missed a few beats. But sitting in the dark with buttered popcorn, watching a film, always seems like the right thing to do.

Our hotel room looked out to San Francisco in the distance behind the Bay Bridge, the Golden Gate a little further beyond to the right. The last night there I worked a little on a short story about a group of kids who fall into the belly of a bridge abutment. I can't get it right. There's always something wrong with it, from one draft to the next. I don't seem to be able to fix it, though I keep trying. I just keep changing the problem.

Just before I fell asleep, I stared at the low moon over the bay and wondered what the American Dream really was. A way to do what you love? A way to make a difference? The luxury to be able to dream? I guess it depends on how fortunate you are.

I listened to the sound of the traffic streaming by on the 580, feeling lucky to have a deep-thinking son (and daughter back home) and a wife who still loves me. They're always teaching me stuff. I thought back to earlier this weekend, when we stopped by a hillside community rose garden in Oakland. The three of us walked the circular path from the road, leading down into a Zen pool at the bottom. We kept stopping by the tall rose bushes and calling each other over to smell the hybrid fragrances: *Typhoo Tea, Pink Peace, Beautiful Dreamer.*

This is a dream or I could be lying

You see me in the supermarket
and I lie about the dream,
say it was my father's, not mine.
I'm ashamed and you know it.
I never told you this before,
I say, *but I remember when*
I did something awful.
Then I notice my shopping cart is empty
and I think I see pity on your face.
I watch you roll away
realize the lies are failing me:
the ones I've grown up with,
the ones I've invented,
and a voice in the courtesy booth
asks over the loud speaker,
America, what is happening to you?

III

The City I Left

The city I left
had miles of barrooms
and Italian bakeries
and clam shacks.

The city I left
had poker machines
(that paid off) in the VFWs
and two race tracks
(horses and dogs) and the kids
there gambled their lunch
money in grade school.

The city I left had
Shirley Ave drug runners
and prostitutes
and strip clubs
from the beach to Squire Road.

The city I left had rotating
ethnic neighborhoods
Italian, Jewish, Puerto Rican,
Laotian.

The city I left
was my mother's home
until three years ago,
Lancaster Ave at the foot
of the General Edwards Bridge,
the constant rush of traffic
over the green iron grate,
houses packed in between
single car driveways, dogs

barking, seagulls squawking,
sirens around the corner
day and night.

In the city I left, five stops
on the blue line to Boston,
I saw the last of the carnival
pack up its wagons and leave
the three-mile urban beachfront behind.
I saw the crowded barrooms thin
and die along Broadway.
I saw the gangsters
move to the suburbs
to hide out in their ranch houses
and barbecue steaks
and wash their cars
and plant grass over buried bags of cash.

Learning to Talk

I breathe 1 – 2 – 3, resist
the urge to lecture. He doesn't understand

that I understand, or maybe I don't,
really. We cry, explain ourselves,

and I feel lucky for a moment,
his shoulders cradled in my arms,

not so different from a few years
ago when he lay on my chest

in the shade of the cypresses
at the beach. *It's because I love*

you I say and it sounds honest
but inadequate and it brings us back

to the fact that he is seventeen
and I am fifty-two and that gap

can't always be filled with wisdom
or advice or memory.

Why I Love Basketball

the science—
        speeding spacing driving
three chest passes and a lay-up
        five sets of hands a string theory

the spectacle—
        sneakers squeaking
players elevating
        rim walkers sky dancers
tipping grabbing swatting

the language—
        not in my house
cross over step back hook shot
        back door banking slamming
fast break jamming
        boom boom in your face
(like Shaq might say)
        how's my ass taste

Leitrims Pub—1979

after Kris Kristofferson

The bartender *knew my name,*
ran tabs,
forgave us for throwing
the metal disc too hard
at the bowling machine.

In this place, Greg the accountant
put bets on the horses
and J.D., who looked like Zero
Mostel, had to sleep outside
under a tree every night,
and Dino, who did five-
hundred push-ups a day,
always slid us a free one.

I elbowed up here
the better part of my undergraduate days
drinking buckets of draft beer, playing
gambling games, smoking cigarettes.
To this day I remember more about
the barflies than Irish Drama
or Old English Poetry.

I called my father from the pay phone here
to tell him I wouldn't be graduating,
told him to cancel the hotel room
for him and my grandmother.

After everyone went home that spring,
I sat alone at the end of the bar,
the door open to the *Sunday morning sidewalk*

wishing I could start over,
wishing Lord that I was stoned
not knowing then how many times
I would make this wish again.

After the Celtics

Years later her brother killed his wife and blamed it on a black guy.
The cops believed it and found one.
But this night, I kissed her red lips in a barroom after the Celtics
won a championship. I asked her to take a walk on the beach the next day.
It never happened.

When I heard what her brother did—staged a murder then jumped
off the Tobin Bridge—I thought of her, her nervous smile, her quick laugh.

I wondered what would have happened if we had taken that walk. Would
we have held hands, told jokes, talked about families, the way her brother
was so quiet when they all got together for the holidays as if something
was on his mind?

Holidays

Writing in Starbucks,
a gray winter day,
fighting it (again)—
maybe my mother's death
my new place in the order of things.
I'm thinking this is my last year
coaching basketball after 16 seasons,
and last night putting up Christmas lights
my wife tells me she misses
having little kids. The holidays,
always with the introspection.

As a kid I used to get depressed
the day after Christmas as if
I knew even then the savior was a hoax.
Now I'm not so sure. I pray,
I meditate, sometimes I use rescue spray
in between visits to the homeopath.
Sometimes I believe my prayers are being
answered or my father's prayers were
answered for me (that time in the car).

I want it to be a true story:
a scared little kid at 60 years old
praying for his kids like his father did,
believing what the brothers at St. Johns
told him—
the bank will be open
when you need it most.

On the Eve of My Son's Graduation—
May 2016

I listen to Ravel's *Boléro*
looking out my hotel room window
at the Chicago River
and the folks walking fast on West Wacker.
It's still 45 degrees in May
the flags blowing,
the skateboarders in hoodies,
the skyline boasting against the blue:
The Wrigley Building
The Chicago Tribune
and the gaudy Trump Tower
behind the Wabash Avenue bridge
like a dictator's totem—
a modern-day *Metropolis*.
This is what it's come to—
fiction as truth, angry mobs
(righteous and otherwise),
and the media sprinkling flakes
into the tank.
Here my son: Happy Graduation.

The bow slides across the cello skin
behind me like deep rivers of grief
and a part of me wishes
that we just get it over with
that the buildings out my window
slip into the water one by one,
the brick and the steel and the mortar
all lumped into the blue green current
and heading out to Lake Michigan,
leaving nothing but the empty streets

and the panhandlers and the one tattooed kid
on his cell phone posting a picture
of the smoldering rubble on Snapchat
with a caption that says *finally.*

Orphan

There will come a day
in a retreat house in New Jersey
when an orphan ghost
passes by your window

you will hear a hum
the clang of a radiator
someone whispering

you will feel the rush
of cool air
under your door
the rough sheets on your legs

you will hear one foot
pressing on the wooden floor
then another

and for a moment
it will all make sense
the gaunt child standing
with a smirk on his face

the bony hand
pulling the blankets
from your feet.

The Kid

*

The Kid stands
in the schoolyard,
his sister and the others circling him
yelling *fight fight fight.*

*

The Kid dribbles a basketball,
fast and reckless, always shooting—
a new Wilson every Christmas morning
stuck in a frozen rope net.

*

The Kid loves the gyms, the sneakers squeaking,
the sweat, the sound of tickled twine.

*

Soon *the others* come calling
(they all do it)
so the Kid does it too,
under the bridge on summer nights
dark light basement hideouts
and later, shoddy clubs in the combat zone.

*

Soon the Kid becomes that guy on the beach,
the duck toy, paddle feet, wobbling home
singing a song or cursing at something,
you know him *good guy but* . . .

*

The Kid prays (like his father did)
but the mistakes cling to him
like dryer lint,
more of them washing up every day
in the noon gray tide.

*

The family knows now . . .
They want to yell
get the Kid out of the game.

*

The Kid knows it's almost over.
He's too far gone to come back.

*

The Kid stands
where the schoolyard used to be.
Makes up some story about
why it is the way it is—
they don't understand . . .
The hoops are gone, there's condos now.
A flock of pigeons circles
in the winter sky.

Stopping and Starting

In elementary school I was lost,
stuttering my way through reading,
the snickers, the jokes,
trying to avoid
the kids flicking cigarettes
against the schoolyard wall,
the ones who would later
burn down the boatyard
or follow someone's sister into the marsh.

The basketball court saved
me for a while,
switching hands to the hoop,
crossing over for a foul line
jumper, but already the others
were calling with their booze
and their dope.

I used to always say, *but I
wasn't a bad guy,* something I
held onto for a long time. *I got
trapped,* I told my kids one night,
*and before I knew it,
I was thirty years old.*

But I never stopped playing
the game I loved, never lost
those days on the playground
when I felt whole,
when I had a purpose.
I kept that good first step,
that hard dribble,
stopping and starting
enough to survive.

The Hulk Gets Angry

Another tantrum? *No.*
Do you even realize what you look like
stomping down the street
in your ripped shorts,
big balled fists smashing
everything in sight,
grunting like a man lifting walls?
Who was it this time,
the arrogant soldier,
a politician calling for your head,
another rock monster of molecular density?
I'd like to think injustice made you lose it all.
Ya right.
Look at you
dumb, confused,
the dust and the rubble
all around you *(everywhere you go)*,
an always innocent
puny white human
in a torn dress shirt
still drunk from the power.

The Last Party

Folks from the beach came too, cousins I hadn't seen since the days working the bar. Old friends, some co-workers, some poets. We ate crackers and cheese, ziti, sliced beef. There was coffee and tea, a mountain of chocolate squares and cream-filled cannoli. The bar was open in the corner. The younger kids started a game of tag on the dance floor. They kept sneaking up behind me. I made the rounds at each table, talked about my mom to her neighbors. *She had a good run.*

An old pal came by—*remember the time we hit every bar on the beach?*

One by one people wished us well, found their coats, and left. It all seemed to happen too quickly, a celebration of someone's life.

I put my arm around my sister. *We're not on deck anymore,* I said.

My daughter was sad, losing her last grandparent. I remembered taking her to visit in the nursing home a few weeks before and saying, *if I have to go to a place like this . . . please just push me in front of a bus.*

She nodded okay.

But not next week, I said, *I haven't finished watching* Fargo *yet.*

Coach

Nineteen years ago, I started coaching
a seventh-grade boys basketball team.
I gave it up this year. This would
have been my first day of practice.
The first day of running two-line lay-ups,
whistling starts for wind sprints,
the leather ball bouncing in my hands
to demonstrate a crossover dribble,
or bending my knees for a free throw clinic.
(I always missed the first one of the season.)
What I'm feeling is not unfamiliar—
it's like the day my daughter said she wasn't
going to play basketball anymore.
I understood, of course, the game had passed
her by some—she would have been a junior
playing J.V. No one wants that.
But my heart sank the same way,
knowing I wouldn't be sitting in the stands
at some other high school watching her
running up and down the court, playing tough
defense, hitting that jump shot she liked
(side of the key from fifteen). *Have you
consulted me about this decision?* I asked.
I think of my father watching me, all those
car rides to different gyms, sweaty guys packed in
the back seat. I yelled in the stands for my
daughter like he did for me. I will always
remember coaching that championship YMCA team,
or the next year when we, the underdogs, almost beat
the bigger older girls in the playoffs, a rebound
and a last-second shot outlasting us.
I should have called time-out earlier,

I said after. The coach's ever-present lament.
And those seventh-grade boys, a few hundred
games worth with them, and the ones I can't forget,
a 5'10" kid getting 12 rebounds against two guys 6'4"
(another almost win) or the kid we called *Bingo*
after he curled off a pick to hit a game-winning bank
shot at the buzzer, or that last game, the team's decision
to keep feeding the weakest player on our team
because he hadn't scored yet this year,
even though we were in a 3-point game.
I loved pacing the sideline yelling encouragement,
occasionally drawing the attention of a referee,
scribbling Xs and Os even when the execution
on the court looked nothing like it. It was
never about being the best—it was about
getting kids to play for each other. To take pride
in being a team. To love the game. It's a great game.
One day soon someone I haven't seen in a while
will call me *Coach,* and even though it's over
I will nod. I've earned a ticket into that club and
they're not kicking me out yet.

Sundays

His religion.
A long row of wooden stools.
Two decks of butts and a short stack of cash.
The old man at a table behind him making book,
people dropping money on the way by,
picking up envelopes from the week before.
At the stick, a large round man,
a nicotine-stained voice, calling out folks by name,
and a younger brother, a cop then too, in uniform,
patting some backs before kickoff,
and a roofer telling that one again
about falling three stories
and flapping his arms like wings.
The place is dark and loud and smoky,
and he sits for twelve hours:
three football games,
one late lunch,
five games of darts,
and there's always an after party
and crashing on someone's couch
and calling in sick the next morning (again)

the hungover pagan,
spilling his thick blood onto a stone.

The Wake

Billy King is dead.
OxyContin
Thirty-eight.
Lived with Grandma.
Liked to gamble.
Liked to laugh.
Smiled always.
Shook your hand.
Said things like
hi-O and *whackout.*
Drank Budweiser.
Liked the dogs.
Fried the clams.
Walked the beach.
Told jokes.
One of the good guys.

I hear someone in line behind me:
He looks okay in the box:
Not too bloated.
Not too dead.

A Long Line

I come from a long line
of beachfront vendors
caramel popcorn hawkers
bartenders fry cookers

A long line of coffee pushers
Crackerjack stumpers
cheeseburg makers

A long line of sawdust-
footed hotdog-dragging
cigarette-smoking
liquor-swabbing drink men

I come from a long line
of weary waiters
thumping home
after 8 hours in the box
three a.m. tired-eyed
half-in-the-wrapper
drink pourers

A long line of sidewalk sweepers
cash collectors
grill scrapers
counter wipers
ashtray-emptying
straw box-stuffing
roast beef-slicing
French fry bag-stacking
barroom-bouncing beach bums

Another long day another short buck
Hawk it loud and proud friend

Long days

Long nights

A long line of late-day sleepers

The Morning After the New York City Young Filmmakers Festival—May 2018

For Phil Levine

In the East Village
the city wakes

garbage trucks grinding
bikers on a green asphalt path

walkers left and right
dissolving into each other

the sun hits the former tenement
buildings, makes shadows off the fire escapes

big Zs up and down
each brick and stuccoed canvas

every once and a while
it gets quiet

like everyone has been stopped
at a gate I can't see

a mass of people, cars and trucks
and bikes all idling behind a stop sign

waiting for permission
to return to the commute,

and here they come:
zoom, swish, grind

here they come
and never stop.

Later in the Egg Shop
on Kenmare and Elizabeth

I listen to a Marshall Tucker song
on the speakers around me

waiting for my maple sausage
and biscuit

it's 80 degrees, the doors open
construction workers on the sidewalk out front

the city in full swing now and I think
about my life writing, teaching

coming here to see a film my son edited
and it brings me back

to another time when I wanted
to disappear

and I know how easy that is
just to float over the table

step through the Sheetrock dust
on the sidewalk

sneak along the boulevard
with a suitcase

hop a train and vanish into a city
like another customer

another construction worker
another biker

another tattooed wait server
another cab driver

another homeless man
another mixed-up kid with a two-wheeler

lugging cases of soda
down into dark sidewalk cellars

and Toy Caldwell lays into a lyric like I'd seen
on an episode of *Nashville Now*

and it carries over the late morning sun
like an anthem to this city

and there I am not turning back
riding a southbound . . . till the train it run out of track.

Hovering

There's my father walking from the blue
line station down the colosseum steps
of City Hall Plaza, one careful leg at a time,
on his way to the courthouse
where he takes prisoners upstairs
and says *all rise* to the court in session.
His knees are thick with worry,
the daily struggle reminds him
of his unsettled children, the steps
a kind of suffering he will take
later to the Arch Street church
spend his lunchtime kneeling
with prayers for all of us.
Was there a moment when I could feel
them, their touch on my shoulders,
a shake or a shudder I couldn't explain—
a car accident, a big mistake, more
than my share of close calls?
Years later I walk these same steps
thinking of him—I don't mean
the post-college drunk walk after hours
in the Bell in Hand, or screaming with
a crowd of Celtics fans in '81 when Larry Bird
trash talks Big Mo in front of a championship
banner, but much later, as a parent myself,
an ordinary fall day, a paper cup of tea in my hand,
well past the morning shuffle,
the cool air blowing from the harbor
on Atlantic Ave, the empty plaza at rest,
and I think of those mornings
he struggled to walk on the cement
as worn as his aching knees,

each swollen step,
each thankless hour of worry and duty
draped on him like a curse,
and all those prayers he said
hovering overhead
looking for their station.

Nothing

What's the worst that could
happen?

Nothing?

no feeling
no sight,
no breath,
no choir of angels
or army of saints,
no reception line of family
and friends,
no bright lights,
no peace,
no thing

I'd like to believe I get
a say, come back
six-foot-nine with a long range
jump shot,
an early first round pick,
the next Francis Ford
Coppola or James Baldwin,
or Elvis before the pills,
or maybe just me again,
a little wiser,
a little stronger,
a little less afraid of it all.

House Call

For Julius Erving

Smoother than an Orange Julius,
flying over the rim
like a 747 over downtown Philly,
like a crop duster
like a piper cub through the mountains—
was that The Doctor?
The ABA the NBA
short shorts and long socks
an afro swaying in the altitude
maybe a finger roll to save you face
(before it was a thing)
maybe not,
maybe a big swooping dunk
from the mean fast-break machine.
You trying to choke out a win against Bird
beating my Celtics with your *up and unders*
with your foul line J's
with your smooth rising silk,
and before that
a college kid at a basketball camp,
standing flat-footed under the basket,
rising and dunking two balls at once.
I was sitting under that hoop watching you,
while you stayed in the air for a week
before touching down
before answering your house call.
On my bedside radio, Johnny Most called you *Julius*
but we all knew you were *The Doctor*,
a shimmy here, a shimmy there
lifting, soaring, extending,
a solo flight in the empty sky.

Just Visiting

For Peanuts, the greatest barber on the beach

I see your face somewhere beneath
the gray sunken cover
a side of your head I've never seen
like a temple slumped into itself.
Your swollen arms shake when I touch you,
all your tired body in reverse.

I watch you take each breath
like the burdened believer
waiting for the soul to rise.
You reach up and touch my face.
We are alone and I tell you
it will be okay and I feel
like a liar feels.

I want to tell you to not be afraid
but I am no one who has that right.

I kiss your forehead and rub
your scalp and say good-bye
and only the twinkled traces of
morphine linger in your stare
and you close your eyes
and go to sleep for now.

Another Ending

I heard a story on the news
about a father who
drove over his kid
backing out of his driveway.
The kid was hiding
under a pile of leaves.
In the last seconds
of his life he said
Daddy, I can't breathe.
It's a scene I can't get
out of my mind:
a cul-de-sac
a white clapboard house
blacktop driveway
basketball hoop
some smoke
from a brick chimney
a young father holding
his dying child
the trees swaying
in the fall breeze
the sky full of gray clouds
the car engine still running.

Acknowledgments

These poems have appeared in the following places, some in a slightly different form:

Academy of American Poets—Poem a Day: "Set in Stone"
Allegro Poetry Magazine: "Night Swimming, Assumption College—1979"
Dime Store Review: "Hovering"
Fledgling: Rumney Marsh Press: "Just Visiting"
Junto Magazine: "Reunion"
LIPS: "Not Tonight"
The Paterson Literary Review: "Charlestown Boy's Club
      Tournament—1979," "Concord," "The Curse," "The Hulk Gets
      Angry," "The Kid," "Learning to Talk," "Leitrims Pub—1979,"
      "Memory," "Orphan," "Picking Up the Trail," "Stopping and
      Starting," "Sundays," and "Super Blue Boy"
Poets of the Palisades (2020): "A Dream in Newark" and "Thirteen Ways of
      Looking at a Blackboard"
The Seventh Quarry Poetry Magazine (Swansea): "Anna Maria Island,"
      "This is a dream or I could be lying," and "West Palm"
Tiferet: Fostering Peace through Literature & Art: "The Tobin Bridge"

Special thanks to my poetry peeps in Salem and Beverly, MA, Salem State University, and the Salem Writers, especially JD Scrimgeour, Jan O'Neil, Jennifer Martelli, MP Carver, Cindy Veach, Colleen Michaels, and Lis Horowitz. Thanks also to Sean Thomas Dougherty and Jeffrey Renard Allen for their support and friendship. And thanks to my poetry friends in New Jersey (from Paterson to Madison) RG Evans, Mark Hillringhouse, Maria Mazziotti Gillan, and Laura Boss, and thanks to my friends at the FDU/

MFA program and the poet Bill Zander, RIP. Thanks also to CavanKerry Press, Joan Cusack Handler, Gabriel Cleveland, and to Joy Arbor and Baron Wormser for being the wonderful editors that they are. Thanks to my family, Betty, Kevin, and Michaela for their support and inspiration, and to my longtime friend Ed Boyle who reads almost everything I write.

CavanKerry's Mission

CavanKerry is committed to expanding the reach of poetry and other fine literature to a general readership by publishing works that explore the emotional and psychological landscapes of everyday life and relationships.

Other Books in the Emerging Voices Series